Listening
A RESPONSE ABILITY

Listening
A RESPONSE ABILITY

by Loretta Girzaitis

Illustrations by Pat Ryan

A special UPPER ROOM edition
published by arrangement with
St. Mary's College Press, Winona, Minnesota

Listening—A Response Ability
© 1972 by St. Mary's College Press, Winona, Minnesota

A special edition arranged for distribution by The Upper Room, Nashville, Tennessee

ACKNOWLEDGMENTS

The advertising firm of Campbell-Mithun, Inc., Minneapolis, in the fall of 1970 ran an ad in *TIME* magazine which capsulized the ideas in this book. Permission has been granted by them to use the photo and copy on pages 112 and 113.

The quotation on page 45 is reprinted with permission of the Religious Public Relations Council, Inc., Riverside Drive, New York City.

PHOTO CREDITS

Brother Michael Amengual, FSC—page 54

John Arms—pages 24-25

Gerry Armstrong—pages 34, 38, 56, 57, 58

Jerry Bushey—pages 14, 21, 71, 76

Camelot Communications—pages 83, 106

Frank Cole—page 110

Chicago Tribune—cover, page 105

Duane Delich—page 102

Loretta Girzaitis—pages 16, 19, 28, 40, 52, 53, 66, 67, 68, 70, 84, 85, 88, 91, 98, 99, 101, 103, 109

Bernie Greene—pages 13, 48-49

Hi-Time Publishers, Inc.—page 51

Phil Kaczorowski—pages 9, 69, 108

J. Landy Photos—page 80

Jean-Claude LeJeune—pages 72-73, 75, 86-87

Dick Mann—page 65

Minneapolis Tribune—page 59, 96-97

Steve Murray—pages 15, 22, 23, 79

Jeffrey Piepho—page 107

Norman Provost, FSC—pages 31, 37, 62, 93

Tom Salyer—page 24

Owen Schmidt—page 32

David Schultz—page 100

First Printing—July 1972
Second Printing—October 1973
Third Printing—March 1975

ISBN: 0-88489-047-3
Library of Congress Card Catalog #72-77722

CONTENTS

This book is dedicated

to U
whose lives have touched mine
and
to U
whom I have touched.

SEEKING TOGETHER

Let us, you and I, lay aside all arrogance.
Let neither of us pretend to have found the truth.
Let us seek it as something unknown to both of us.
Then we may seek it with love and sincerity
    when neither of us has the rashness nor
        presumption to believe that he already
        possesses it.
And if I am asking too much of you,
    allow me to listen to you at least,
        to talk with you as I do with beings whom,
for my part,
    I do not pretend to understand.

St. Augustine

St. Augustine truly sets a climate, an atmosphere of openness, when he suggests that neither you nor I, as we spend time together, presume to possess the full truth.

Reflecting, checking out where we are, where we have come from, and where we are going can be an exhilarating adventure. Each of us stands at a specific point in our personal histories. And because you and I have created our own special sounds, we must learn to listen to each other. We must develop a specific competence—that of RESPONSE ABILITY.

However, this skill of responding one to another is impossible unless a relationship exists. In its simplest, a relationship is the manner in which a person stands alongside an-other, the state by which he is mutually interested in the other. Yet this position or this interest is not sufficient. There must be a link of one to another.

A letter of the alphabet, as it stands alone, un-linked, unconnected, is but a letter. We must take the letter and place it in a position next to another letter, and another, and another. The relationship of each of these letters forms a word and so begins to make sense, to have meaning.

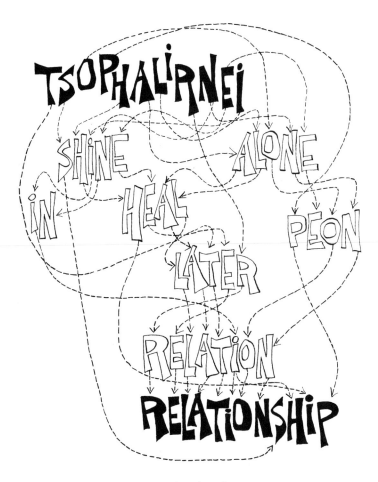

Yet each time we juggle the letters into new positions, the new words carry a new message because the letters keep establishing a new relationship.

So it is with our lives. We begin making sense
when we take our personal islands and extend
them into peninsulas. Then, using the isthmus
as a link, we risk taking the letter *I* to place
it alongside the letter *U*. We establish the vital
connection. The power of response begins to flow,
energizing both letters. Life takes on meaning.

Once this happens, juggling our letters to form
new word patterns is THE adventure, for listening
to the Word which you and I are leads to
RESPONSE ABILITY.

This is what this book is all about. Not about
responsibility as obligation but RESPONSE
ABILITY as the power to juggle self alongside
other selves. It is the competence to listen to
life, to experience, to people, so as to answer
them, to embrace them, to incorporate them into
self as total meaning.

WHAT'S IT ALL ABOUT?

CONVERGENCE

CAPACITY → ABILITY CITY

PART 1

Each person carries within himself
ABILITY, which is the seed of power.
Each cultivates this seed and brings it
to fruition in his own special way.
If his ability is a power or force
to sway or control others,
then the relationship,
the manner in which such a person
stands alongside an-other,
is one of
domination.

John, who received everything he wanted as a child
and who is now a wealthy bachelor,
is power-ful.
His money is his weapon and
he wields it as a hand grenade
to blast his way into playboy clubs,
state dinners,
the best hotels, and
swanky barrooms.
The I that he is
wavers unsteadily on a line above,
as he attempts to juxtapose himself
alongside the U
of the others down below.

The attempt is a terrifying one for him,
since it means that once he places himself
on the same level with the other,
his dominion is over.
He stops controlling the scene.
He becomes an equal.
At that point the I,
for John,
must take on new meaning,
since it has moved into a different relationship
with the U.
This is John's crucial moment of truth.
He possesses the ability
to use this truth-ful moment,
if and how he wants to.

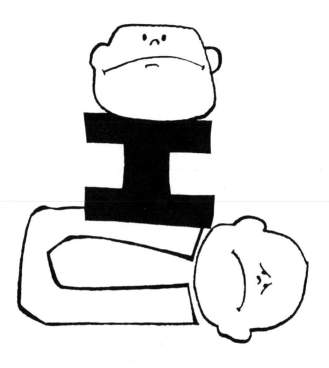

If a person's ability is the power
to act or to perform,
then the relationship,
the manner in which such a person
stands alongside an-other,
is one of achievement.

Doris, a woman executive,
obsessed by the desire for success,
has a compounded problem.
Not only is hers a power of domination,
but it is also a power of disruption.

She fluctuates
in her relationship with others,
sometimes standing above them
and sometimes standing alongside them.
Yet there is very little meaning to her stance.
Depending upon the strength of her desire,
she can trample underfoot
every U that is near her,
stumbling over the shambles she creates.
Doris has a power,
but she no longer controls it.
It controls her.
Her life is out of balance and
if she is to achieve stability,
she must establish new relationships
with all the U's along the way.
But, foremost,
she must discover the relationship
which *I* has with *ME*.

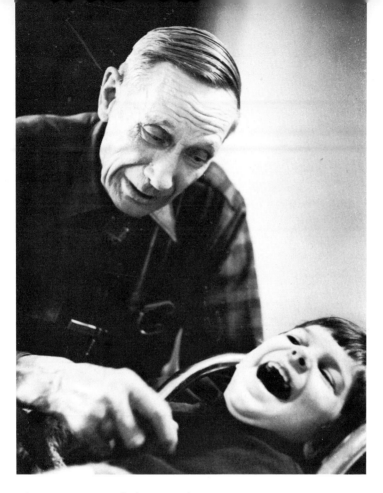

If a person's ability is the power
to respond,
to establish mutually beneficial connections
with others,
then the relationship,
the manner in which such a person
stands alongside an-other
is one of love.

14

Jim was rejected by his peers
because he was "ugly."
He was shuttled from one foster home to another.
When the "what-the-hell" mood hit him,
he was saved from becoming a drug addict
by Alice, a girlfriend who cared.
Today, Jim finds it easy,
not only to stand alongside other U's,
but to put his feet
into their shoes
and to go along the way with them.
Jim has a power,
an ability to understand,
to feel for and with others.
He is not an island,
separate,
apart.
He gently twines himself
into that which is the other
and comes up
with a relationship that has meaning.

Basically,
we all have this power:
the ability to be whatever it is we want to be;
the ability to answer YES or NO
to those walking alongside us;
the ability to establish meaningful relationships;
the ability to listen;
the ability to respond.
Then why is it that so few of us
capitalize upon our abilities?
Could it be
that the capacity within the person is limited?

CAPACITY
is also a power.
Capacity is a receptacle
which is bounded only by the limits
each individual permits.
Capacity is the extent of space
for containing an-other.
It has the ability to receive,
to embrace,
to absorb,
to accept all that an-other has to offer.
And that is where its power lies.

But space is a precious commodity.
Personal space, frequently, is off limits
to others.
Did you ever notice how people shift
when someone gets too close to them?
How they turn their heads away
if a face hovers over their shoulders?
Dancing is an invasion of private space.
When two persons hold each other close
they have opted for sharing their space cushions
with one an-other.
Today's youth are not too eager
for this kind of sharing.
Their dance allows for space barriers and, usually
only arms and legs
can intrude into the territory.
During the liturgy,
some people are terrified,
some resentful,
while others rejoice
at the invasion of private, personal space.
The simple handshake of peace seems
to challenge a person's cushion of private space.

How many people box themselves
into their own personal space sections
and so limit their capacity
to receive?
How many individuals risk being open
by offering space to those
with ability to give?

When?
Where?
How?
Do ability and capacity touch?
Cross boundaries?
Establish a relationship
of balanced giving and receiving?

CONVERGENCE
is the movement
of one object
toward an-other
until both meet.
People converge
to the scene of an accident.
Traffic converges
to the entrance of a freeway.
Firemen converge
to the spot of a fire.
The Minnesota River converges
upon the Mississippi.
As each of these touches the other,
something happens.

When ability converges upon capacity,
an initial response is generated.
One person, fortified by his power,
offers an-other love.
The other, dependent upon his capacity,
accepts it,
or rejects it.
Or, not caring enough to reject it,
he ignores it.
He fails to listen to the person
and acts as if the other and his ability to love
have no value,
no importance.
Here, there is no proper convergence,
for one is giving
but the other is not receiving.

Or it may be that
a person's capacity for receiving
is cavernous.
He constantly craves sympathy.
He demands from others
flattery for his ego
beyond their ability to give.
Here there is no right convergence either,
for one power overbalances the other.

24

Convergence initiates balanced response
when the person with ability
truly respects,
truly listens, and
truly understands
the capacity of the other
and makes no demands.
True respect,
true listening, and
true understanding
are also required of the person
with a great capacity.
It is at this balanced give-receive fulcrum
that the meeting point,
CONVERGENCE,
takes on meaning.
Man begins to realize
his Response Ability to listen
to the other
in the total Word that the other is.

THE NO-THING RESPONSE: PLAYING GAMES of NON-LISTENING

OFF
ON

PART 2

28

Playing games of non-listening
is an amusing pastime
for quite a few of us.
We have
many push-button mechanisms
by which
we turn off
an-other.

We listen with our ears.
Verbal sounds bounce back and forth
on our eardrums.
Sometimes they make sense;
frequently, they don't.
We tune out, turn off
that which we don't want to hear.
We pretend that we are listening
but in our phoniness
we tell the other by our inattentiveness
that he is not really important,
that what he is saying doesn't really matter.
The student does this frequently.
He enters the classroom,
locates himself comfortably,
establishes what he thinks
is an attentive position,
and drifts into the cushioned world
of his fantasies.
A parent does this, too.
But the father's lack of response is quite cruel.
Jack's whistling annoys him.
"Stop it," he growls.
"Can't you see I'm trying to read the paper?"
And the ache inside Jack becomes a gnawing pain.

"He doesn't care about me," Jack mumbles
as he mentally locates another guy
with whom he'll share his problem.
His father failed to listen to the cue
that introduced Jack's need to talk.

We listen with our minds.
As the other presents an idea
we calculate the response.
We find it important to prepare a defense,
marshall an argument,
prove to the speaker
that he doesn't have all the facts.
We debate instead of dialogue.
When the other touches the nerve-endings
of our biases
we become defensive as our pet theories
become threatened.
We fear the change that may come
if we open ourselves honestly
to balancing another's thought with our own.
Once, after a homily I had delivered,
a mother told me that her son had said,
"I don't want to listen."
You see, I had told the audience
that if they listened,
inevitably, they would change
because they would admit into their minds
ideas that had not been there before.
They would have to make choices:
either to accept, reject,
or modify these ideas.
Permitting entrance could be
a dangerous miscalculation.

Ideas are not truly alive
if they are locked in our minds.
When U share an idea with me,
I should not be threatened,
even if the idea is strange to me.
In a sense, I lack freedom
if my ideas are tucked safely in their box
without having been tested by other ideas.
If U present an idea which rocks my value system,
U help me,
for U provide me with an opportunity
to examine my idea,
to re-discover its worth,
or to acknowledge its death.
This is where choice comes in.
I can choose, after evaluating your idea,
to keep mine intact.
Or I can choose to discard mine
and adopt yours.
Or I can modify yours and modify mine
and admit a slightly new version into my own mind.
Regardless of which choice I make,
U have done me a service
for U have popped me like a Jack-in-the-box
out of my cramped quarters
and offered me new alternatives.

We listen with our emotions.
If I do not like the way a person looks,
or if I do not like the tone of his voice,
if I do not like his other differences,
I can get all tied up inside
with anger,
frustration,
rejection,
or even with hatred.
I can pass judgment
and write him off as worthless
or insignificant.
This defensiveness of mine
can be a simple indication
that I am not equipped to decode the message
the other is sending,
that my capacity is limited,
that I will not provide the space
for that which the other is offering.
So I label the other uninteresting
and deny myself
the opportunity
of discovering him.

38

When I am uptight
I cater to my deaf spots
since I feel the other is trespassing
on my most cherished notions and convictions.
I build solid walls by labeling him
insensitive,
uncaring,
unloving.
These walls are thick enough to prevent
me from a confrontation
to really test my assumption.
Yet conflict at this point
could become a healing process.
It could bring about the opportunity
to explore problems together
so as to establish
a balanced relationship

A deaf spot usually emerges
when I feel
that the other is manipulating,
is dominating
the relationship.

But by refusing to listen
I block him off and,
instead,
listen to my own pitiful wailings
as I lick the wounds I refuse
to bandage.
It is when I can state my feelings
without blaming the other;
it is when I can explore
my feelings with the other;
it is when I can overcome
personal threat and insecurity
that I can risk listening.
It is at this point
that convergence takes place
I open myself
to my fullest capacity
and encourage the other
to use his power of giving.
Simultaneously, as we keep reversing the roles
in this give-and-take,
we begin to understand each other.

We listen with our hearts.
When I listen with the heart
I stop playing the game of non-listening.
In other words,
I step inside the other's skin;
I walk in his shoes;
I attempt to see things from his point-of-view;
I establish eye contact;
I give him conscious attention;
I reflect my understanding of his words;
I question;
I attempt to clarify.
Gently,
I draw the other out
as his lips stumble over words,
as his face becomes flushed,
as he turns his face aside.
I make the other feel that
I understand that he is important,
that I am grateful that he trusts me enough
to share deep, personal feelings with me.
I grant him worth.

When I tell you that I love you,
are you embarrassed?
frightened?
responsive?
Do you think of sex?
understanding?
warmth?
support?
God?
or none of these?
What *meaning* do U give the word *love*?
How different is it
from the meaning that I give it?
"I
know
you believe
you understand
what you think
I said
but I am not sure
you realize
that what you heard
is not what I meant."

PART 3

Listening is a risky enterprise,
for it implies that a person recognizes
the perils that this involves.
When I listen,
not simply hear noise vibrations,
but really listen, then I set aside
my limitations,
my hangups,
my inhibitions,
my terms
and respond to the need of the other.
My capacity must be "stretchy" enough
to expand,
to extend,
to reach out to contain
that which an-other offers.
A listening heart does not focus
on the cost of such an effort
nor on the pain that may ensue
if the risk boomerangs.
Its main concern is
to increase its capacity
to accept.

Yet before I can listen to an-other
I must learn to listen to myself.
I must first discover who I am,
what my abilities are,
what kinds of capacities I possess.
I must determine,
not my limitations,
but my possibilities.
So many times I am stymied
because my capacity is restrained
by my limited vision.
I refuse to concede to myself
that there are really no boundaries
to what I may become.
Do I fear to listen to myself, however,
because the acknowledgment
of an unlimited expansion of my finiteness
may place demands upon me
that may do havoc to ego-veneration?

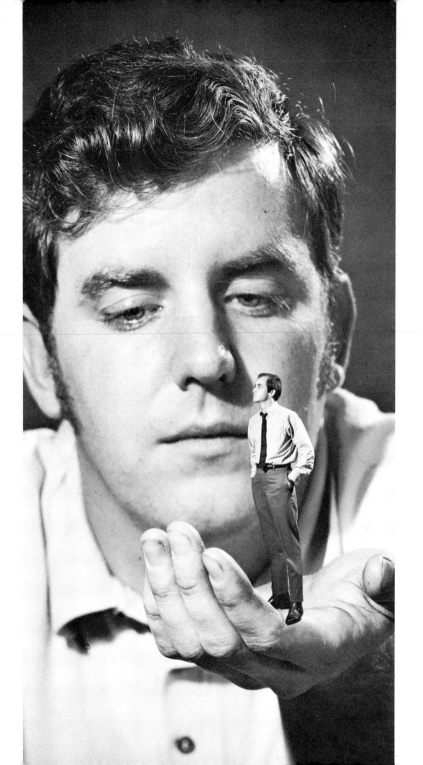

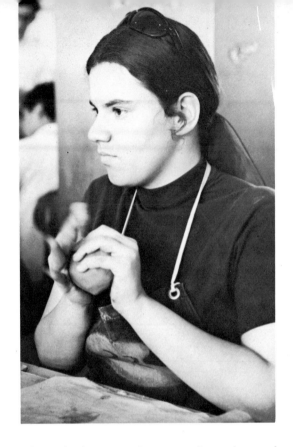

If, with the conclusion of my formal education,
I withdraw from conscious awareness
of my experiences,
my skills, and
my talents
then I become content with the status of
that moment. I become as a lump of clay
that others mold or buffet at will.
I cannot determine my own destiny
because I have ceased
to listen to my own heartbeat.

A beautiful story tells us that eons ago
God shaped mud into a form,
that He stamped upon it His own image
and likeness. Do I believe this? Really?
If I am made to God's image and likeness,
then I must possess,
in some measure,
His beauty, His goodness, His love-ableness,
His love-ability.
If I believe this,
then I should be able, easily,
to list five beautiful things about myself.
Not superficial, exterior things,
but the core things that do make me
His image and likeness.
Can I admit that daily I live a life,
enjoy experiences, respond to events,
in such a way that my image and likeness of Him
become more and more apparent?

54

How do I listen to others when they praise me?
when they tell me of the good I do?
when they highlight my capacity
to love,
to respond,
to be warm?
Do I brush it off
as flattery,
or as insignificant?
Do I become embarrassed?
Do I deny, protest that all this is nothing?
Or do I listen to this feedback
and see reflected the image of God that others,
perhaps unconsciously,
perceive?
Can I lift my heart in worship,
in gratitude,
and accept, in truth,
that which others say I am?
Few people can stand to hear
what they ought to hear.
Can my prayer become:
"Dear God, help me to see the truth about myself—
no matter how beautiful it might be."

So many of us live our lives
full of fear and negation.
Daily
we beat our breasts
in sorrow and discouragement
as our lists of failings and weaknesses
fill ever-expanding columns.
Suppose that for the next week or two
instead of reviewing our failings
we list all the beautiful things we do each day
and then thank God
that we have capitalized
on daily opportunities
to become more
His image and likeness.

Quite a few of us
recoil from this suggestion,
for it seems to smack of pride.
Yet what is humility?
Is it simply the listing of evils within us?
Is it brow-beating our egos?
or is humility
TRUTH?
an acknowledgment of the balances within us?
Am I a more genuine person because
I acknowledge my sinfulness
but ignore my capacity for good?
Am I more God's image
if I live as if evil had triumphed—
or was about to triumph?

Then what was Jesus all about?
If I listen to what He had to say
when He took on God's image for man,
then I can learn
fascinating things
about myself.
He declared that
the second greatest commandment is
to love your neighbor AS YOU LOVE YOURSELF.
Have I ever really heard that commandment before?
He commands me
TO LOVE MYSELF.
He *commands* me
to make that love of self
the standard
by which to love my neighbor.

Just what is my capacity for loving myself?
Can I begin listening to myself,
to every nuance of every thought, every desire,
every act, every feeling
to discover my love-ableness?
And then when I discover
this love-ableness and ACCEPT it,
what do I do next?
Can I ever ignore my Response Ability
to listen to myself constantly
so that I might continue to discover
the image that is ME?
It seems that if I believe I am
God's image and likeness
I have but one alternative:
to use my love of myself as my measuring stick.
How awesome this is, for the way I love myself
is the way that I will love my neighbor.

THE TRUST RESPONSE:

PART 4

The world is full of lonely people,
each isolated in his secret dungeon.
Periodically they send faltering messages
desperately hoping that someone will decode
their communiques of desperation.
If no one responds,
they continue living their private hells,
never really discovering their own beauty
nor the unlimited possibilities that are theirs.

Yet if someone is listening,
extraordinary things begin to happen.
Dungeon walls disappear when
someone stretches out a hand,
whispers a word of encouragement,
attempts to understand.
The prisoner's resistance crumbles
as he begins to hope.
His capacity stretches to include within it
that which the other offers.
Trust becomes the convergence point
as expectation and acceptance meet.
Heart responds to heart
and sets in motion a chain reaction
that generates continuing development and growth.

Once walls disintegrate,
it is easier to get about the business
of establishing the U-I relationship.
Since each is a mystery,
neither has the right
to become possessive of the other.
Each must respect
the uniqueness that the other is.
There can be no prying into secrets,
no pressure to comply to the wishes of the other.
I do not have the right to say,
"If U love me, U will do as I say."
I must respect U as U are
and not attempt to change U
into my own or somebody else's image.
I must be the trampoline upon which U can rest
or can bounce about exuberantly.
Yet, our relationship cannot be lopsided.
U must provide the same climate
of acceptance, trust, and availability for me.

To listen to each other,
to discover the Word that each is,
we must listen to the silences
as well as the sounds
that enmesh our lives together.
For silence has a language all its own.
After celebrating an anniversary together,
a man and a woman need not speak at all.
Yet their silence communicates the
warmth, tenderness, and the exquisite joy,
not only of that one experience
but also of the thousands of memories
of a life lived together.

Jane has displeased her father
and so
to punish her
he ignores her.
"Dear Dad,"
she cries,
"I'm listening,
and your silence is killing me."

Silence is communication,
but when it is intended to
puzzle or manipulate an-other,
it is cruel.
Then it is the spur that turns the other away
and leads the manipulator
into the trap of his own loneliness.
When silence is understanding,
it beckons gently
and calms unruly fears.
It instills confidence and assurance.
It provides the certain knowledge
that the other cares.

One day I was visiting my friend Alice
and as we talked,
her three-year old daughter
came into the living room.
She began nudging her mother.
Turning to her daughter, Alice said,
"Marie, this is mother's quiet time."
Without a word, Marie returned to her toys.
"What was that all about?" I asked.
Alice smiled.
"Every day each of us has our quiet time,"
she said. "When it is our quiet time,
no one is allowed to interrupt.
Each of us has learned to respect
the other's quiet time.
I never interrupt Marie or Tommy
during their quiet time,
so they never interrupt me when I have mine."
This kind of silence, too,
is true of Response Ability.
It insures a period of peace,
of aloneness,
for each member of the family,
which is the space so necessary
to recoup one's energies,
one's thoughts.

Sound, too, is communication.
As sounds patter around us,
we should recognize that
talk is frequently a cover-up
for fears,
insecurities,
petitions to be understood.
At a party,
cocktail conversations are the rule.
Yet, if I stay awhile
and listen to your chatter
the chances are that U may share
an insight,
an observation
that has some value to U.
If I am truly listening,
I will be able to clear away
all the word-debris
and get a glimpse of that
which is U.
If I am tuned in,
I will feel your feeble attempts
as U reach out to touch me.

73

We touch each other
in mysterious ways.
Our vocabulary
is full of the word "touch."
"Let's stay in touch,"
I say as U leave me.
"Because U
have touched me,
I have grown,"
U whisper after
an encounter together.
"What a touching
experience," I marvel
after a theater play,
or a beautiful sunset,
or after a personal
revelation.

74

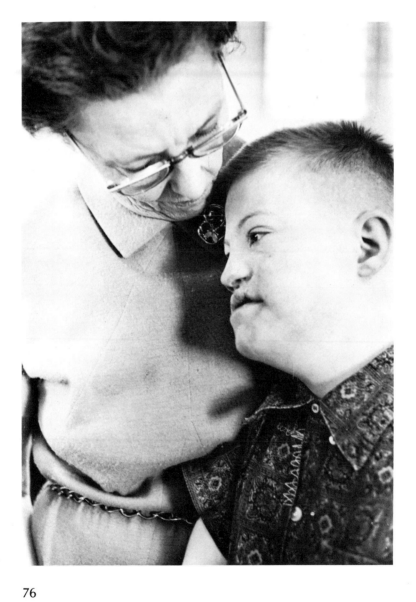

Physical touch is non-verbal communication that,
at times, shouts louder than any words.
A warm handshake,
a squeeze of the shoulder,
an embrace
shatter private space in such a way
that ability and capacity converge
and response is instantaneous.
This is listening
where U and I are
open and
unafraid—
if only for a moment.

Lives are touched in other ways also.
A group of teens took some inner-city children
to a shopping mall at Christmas time.
From their own savings
they gave each child a dollar.
The youngsters were there,
not to buy something for themselves,
but to choose a gift for their parents.
After their shopping spree,
the group celebrated with a wrapping party
and refreshments.
All the way down the line
from teen to child to parent
the pulse of listening love
touched
and
enriched
lives.

In another instance, Dr. Milton,
a suburban general practitioner,
has touched numerous lives,
for he has learned how to listen
to the needs of people.
He has inaugurated Thankmas Day
and set aside December 10
as the day on which to give a gift to someone
as a response to a particular need.
The gift can be a
listening ear,
a favor,
an errand,
a money contribution,
a visit,
the sharing of one's time,
the cancellation of a debt.
But that's not all there is to it.

One of the rules of the game
is that there are to be no thank-you notes.
Instead, the one receiving the gift must,
through listening,
discover another's need
and express his gratitude for the gift received
by giving a gift to that other.
The doctor believes
that Thankmas Day should become
an integral part of the welfare system
so that the indigent need not feel so obligated
and so guilty
because society is helping him out.
If, on Thankmas Day, I cancel a debt
the needy owes me,
his Response Ability lies,
not in thanking me,
but in touching the life of an-other
who, too, has a need.
This kind of listening
lodges demands upon each of us
that touch the core of our beings.
Once I reach out to U
it is inevitable that I touch U,
for I am placed in a specific relationship
with U,
and if we listen to each other
we will discover beauties that otherwise
frequently remain undiscovered.

Words have their own symphony of sound
if orchestrated correctly.
Renee and Jim are a young married couple
who share deeply.
They wait up for the New Year
in a very special way.
On New Year's Eve
Renee makes the best meal of the year
and both eat at midnight by candlelight.
Then they review the year that has just gone by
to see how they have helped each other grow.
The I-U relationship takes on special meaning
as each explores the points of contact
each has had with the other.
Eventually, each examines
the personal growth of the I.
Finally, both share with each other
needs as they see them
for the coming year
and decide how each can respond to them
personally
and with one another.

Let's take a look at the possibility
of another word symphony.
What would happen, if at the next meal,
U were to turn to one of the children and say,
"Joyce, what do U like about yourself?"
The chances are there might be stunned silence,
embarrassment, giggling,
or any other number of responses.
But if U gently pressure the girl
she might be able to tell U what
she likes about herself.
Or, if she could not, then maybe U could lead her
to discover it with your gentle help.
Once she shares it,
then go around the table and
have each member tell Joyce
what each likes about her.
Joyce will grow ten feet tall
as the realization hits her
that her family really likes her.

But don't stop there.
The next night give another child
the same opportunity.
Do this until every member of the family
has had his chance to be on center stage.
U, yourself, share what U like about yourself
and listen as your family tells U
what they like about U.
This seems like a difficult, way-out task.
Yet why?
We take it for granted that,
in the process of growing up,
children must fight and argue with one another.
Why can't we take it for granted, also,
they they should grow up
complimenting and
liking one another?
How much listening takes place
when people argue with one another?
when people compliment one another?

Then there are Dick and Laura
who have reached the agreement
that if one feels
the other has been shut out,
cut off,
he/she will tell the other
"Right now I need tender loving care,"
and the other will respond accordingly.
Their intimate I-U world was shattered
one day when,
quite unexpectedly,
one of the children whispered,
"Right now I need TLC."
So they have opened up their world
to include that of all of their children.
Now everyone listens
and responds
to the cry,
"I need TLC."

Helen and John have also developed
their own communications design.
Their plan ensures open avenues of response
to forestall unnecessary word explosions
at the end of the day.
When John gets home from work
he greets the family
and then Helen and he take off
to their own room
where both discuss the day's events,
the good
and the not-so-good happenings.
By ventilating their feelings,
by airing frustrations,
by sharing the day's joys
they clear the emotional atmosphere
for a tension-less, enjoyable dinner.
The children recognize that
dad's first half hour at home is with mother
and relax in their own way.

Listening to the Words that people are
provides each of us with the opportunity
to develop understanding
not only of the other,
but also of self.
The interaction of response
is the dynamism
that propels me
toward the other
and so we meet, we converge,
in truth,
and love,
and joy.
Yet there are those who, because
of fear,
insecurity, or
pain
flee the I-U convergence point.
In a sense, many of us
sign our death warrants
when we refuse to live
in response to others.
Some of us are like the young woman,
not yet out of her teens,
who wrote the poem on the following page.

An open book am I.
I sell myself
to people
or a
person,
like a can of motor oil.
Black.

Slippery when wet,
crushed when rolled over.
Like a can of motor oil.
Empty . . .
Black.

Love is a faraway island.
Once enjoyed for a time
is gone forever.
Of my own volition, of course.
After all, nobody loves a can of motor oil.
Empty . . .
Crushed . . .
Black.

I am an island hopper.
I have jumped from
Love to love to indifference to hate to
FREEDOM!!

Freedom through disassociation,
cutting ties and bonds,
destroying friendship—
retreating.

Ah! . . . . Bliss!! ?

But the years have been good to her.
In time
her disassociated bliss
has become a warm response.
Today Madge is a loving person,
free,
open,
committed.
Her life was touched by a U
A woman moved
into a redeeming position.
Between Madge and the woman
trust became the convergence point.
Madge's whole world has changed.

THE FOCAL RESPONSE:

I-U-HIM CONVERGENCE POINT

PART 5

"The WORD keeps coming
into the World," emphasizes
Bishop Dozier of Memphis.
But too many of us tune HIM
out. We fail to see the beauty
of the WORD in forests, in
sunsets, in romping animals,
in billowing wheat fields,
in towering peaks.

We fail to see His gentleness
in a soft caress,
a comforting word,
an aged man,
a tiny child,
a star-filled night.

We fail to see His goodness
in the neighbor across the street,
in the policeman at the crossing,
in the priest serving his people,
in those with whom we share our homes,
in the man struggling to be free.

Each of us has our own understanding
of Him, the WORD, whom we call God.
Much of it is dependent
not so much on the words we memorized
about Him, but on the Words to which we have
listened as we grew into maturity.
If the Words around us were those of kindness,
of love,
of understanding,
of compassion
then, as we listened, we responded in kind.
Each of these Words revealed to us
the God
whose image and likeness these people reflected.

But if the Words around us were those
of bitterness,
misunderstanding,
bickering, or
hatred,
then our understanding of the God
these people reflected was one
of harshness,
insensitivity,
aloofness.

It is difficult to know God
since for many of us
He is at the rim of our experience,
of our understanding.
We read about Him.
We listen to others speak of Him.
We see Him reflected around us.
But much of what we see and hear is contradiction.
And so the mysterious
becomes greater mystery.

Jesus, the reflection of the Father,
speaks a hard language
which demands much:
to love God with all of one's capacity;
to love neighbor as self;
to be true, honest, humble,
to become involved.
Listening to his message gives one a jolt.
What happens if I say "Yes"?
Will His demands increase?
Will life take on specific meaning?
Will the price be too costly?
Do I have personal reserves
with which to respond?

What can help me to set determinations
is to stretch spaces in my life
to fill with reflection as I
sit under a hair dryer,
wait for a client,
set a table,
spade a garden,
watch nature,
prepare for dinner.
It is at moments like these that I can listen
to the gentle whisperings within me about
relationships,
life's meaning,
personal values,
attitudes.
I can raise questions that beg answers:
How do I reflect God to others?
How do I see Him reflected in others?
How do I listen to Him?
How do I worship Him?
How do I love?

God does talk.
He speaks through His written revelation.
He speaks through nature,
through His Church,
through every experience,
through every relationship.
His Spirit is all about us,
within us.
The more conscious we become of it,
the more we can respond to it.

God can never be understood in His totality
because if we were to encompass Him,
there would be no reason for our existence.
We possess Him, we reflect Him,
in a very limited way. Yet each day we feel Him,
we see Him, we listen to Him
in everything around us.
As we open ourselves to life, to people,
He shares a bit more of Himself with us.
And so we grow gradually,
sometimes painfully, sometimes joyfully,
to become more His image and likeness
so that others, in turn,
might see Him reflected through us.
Life becomes a glorious adventure
when it has a greater value than mere survival.

When God becomes the focal point,
the center of activity,
the center of attraction,
the center of attention
for U and me,
then the U-I convergence
attains a specific quality.
U and I can listen better to each other,
respond more warmly,
understand each other more adequately,
respect each other truly,
because of that added dimension.

God is the goal toward which I strive,
the dream I attempt to make reality,
the ideal I wish to reflect.
He is the impetus,
the challenge,
the reward.
He is the well-spring
which gives and sustains life.
He is the epitome of
Response Ability.
He contains such power
that He enlivens me to respond to Him.
If my response to Him is honest and true
then U need not fear that my response
to U will be otherwise.

CREATE
IN ME, O GOD,
A
LISTENING
HEART.

Talk can arouse
but of itself
it cannot heal.

To listen—
TRULY listen—
is to begin
the healing process
a wounded nation needs.

Listen to the wind.
Listen to the birds.
Listen to the trees.
Be still,
and listen to your God.

Above all, listen to
your own conscience.
This is the beginning
of listening.

Then,—
listen to one person.
Even for five minutes
each day.

If each of us in the
United States *listened*
with all his might

for just five minutes
each day, wouldn't
we be a healthier nation
for it?

What this country needs
is a good five-minute
listener.

You?